Read for a Better World™

CHICKS
A First Look

ANNA ANDERHAGEN

GRL Consultant, Diane Craig, Certified Literacy Specialist

Lerner Publications ◆ Minneapolis

Educator Toolbox

Reading books is a great way for kids to express what they're interested in. Before reading this title, ask the reader these questions:

> What do you think this book is about? Look at the cover for clues.

> What do you already know about chicks?

> What do you want to learn about chicks?

Let's Read Together

Encourage the reader to use the pictures to understand the text.

Point out when the reader successfully sounds out a word.

Praise the reader for recognizing sight words such as *are* and *in*.

TABLE OF CONTENTS

Chicks 4

You Connect! 21
STEM Snapshot 22
Photo Glossary 23
Learn More 23
Index. 24

Chicks

Baby chickens are called chicks.
They hatch from eggs.

Chicks hatch wet.

Then they get dry and soft.

After they hatch, chicks stay in the nest. Their mom keeps them warm.

How do you stay warm?

Chicks peep to their mom. Their mom clucks back.

Moms teach their chicks how to eat and drink.

Chicks drink lots of water.

What do you like to drink?

Chicks eat worms and bugs.

When they are one week old, they start to fly.

Chicks love to play. They like to look in the mirror.

Why do you think chicks like to look in the mirror?

Chickens can live for ten years or more.

Chicks are very smart!

You Connect!

Have you ever seen a chick?

What is something you like about chicks?

How do you communicate with your family?

STEM Snapshot

Encourage students to think and ask questions like scientists. Ask the reader:

What is something you learned about chicks?

What is something you noticed about chicks in the pictures in this book?

What is something you still don't know about chicks?

Photo Glossary

Learn More

Jopp, Kelsey. *Chicks*. Lake Elmo, MN: Focus Readers, 2020.

Mazzarella, Kerri. *Chickens*. Coral Springs, FL: Seahorse Publishing, 2023.

Neuenfeldt, Elizabeth. *Baby Chickens*. Minneapolis: Bellwether Media, 2023.

Index

drink, 12, 13
eat, 12, 14
fly, 15
mom, 8, 11, 12
nest, 8
play, 16

Photo Acknowledgments

The images in this book are used with the permission of: © Monning27/Shutterstock Images, pp. 4–5, 23 (top right, bottom right); © Nagy-Bagoly Arpad/Shutterstock Images, p. 6; © yevgeniy11/Shutterstock Images, p. 7; © I Wayan Sumatika/Shutterstock Images, pp. 8–9; © Majna/Shutterstock Images, pp. 10–11; © Janice Chen/Shutterstock Images, p. 12; © PUMPZA/Shutterstock Images, p. 13; © pz71/Shutterstock Images, pp. 14, 23 (top left); © TTstudio/Shutterstock Images, p. 15; © ZouZou/Shutterstock Images, pp. 16–17; © HaiGala/iStockphoto, pp. 16, 23 (bottom left); © Tong_stocker/Shutterstock Images, pp. 18–19; © Valentina Razumova/Shutterstock Images, p. 20.

Cover Photograph: © BushAlex/Shutterstock Images

Design Elements: © Mighty Media, Inc.

Copyright © 2025 by Lerner Publishing Group, Inc.

All rights reserved. International copyright secured. No part of this book may be reproduced, stored in a retrieval system, or transmitted in any form or by any means—electronic, mechanical, photocopying, recording, or otherwise—without the prior written permission of Lerner Publishing Group, Inc., except for the inclusion of brief quotations in an acknowledged review.

Lerner Publications Company
An imprint of Lerner Publishing Group, Inc.
241 First Avenue North
Minneapolis, MN 55401 USA

For reading levels and more information, look up this title at www.lernerbooks.com.

Main body text set in Mikado a Medium.
Typeface provided by Hannes von Doehren.

Library of Congress Cataloging-in-Publication Data

Names: Anderhagen, Anna, author. | Craig, Diane, consultant.
Title: Chicks : a first look / Anna Anderhagen ; GRL consultant Diane Craig, Certified Literacy Specialist.
Description: Minneapolis : Lerner Publications, [2025] | Series: Read about baby animals | Includes bibliographical references and index. | Audience: Ages 5–8 | Audience: Grades K–1 | Summary: "Chicks can fly, but what they really love to do most is play. Leveled text and engaging photographs bring young readers up close to the sweet life of baby chickens"—Provided by publisher.
Identifiers: LCCN 2023033625 (print) | LCCN 2023033626 (ebook) | ISBN 9798765626351 (library binding) | ISBN 9798765629475 (paperback) | ISBN 9798765636565 (epub)
Subjects: LCSH: Chicks—Juvenile literature.
Classification: LCC SF498.4 .A53 2025 (print) | LCC SF498.4 (ebook) | DDC 636.5—dc23/eng/20231212

LC record available at https://lccn.loc.gov/2023033625
LC ebook record available at https://lccn.loc.gov/2023033626

Manufactured in the United States of America
1 – CG – 7/15/24